STORMING OF THE BASTILLE

The Start of the French Revolution
History 6th Grade
Children's European History

BABY PROFESSOR
EDUCATION KIDS

Speedy Publishing LLC

40 E. Main St. #1156

Newark, DE 19711

www.speedypublishing.com

Copyright 2017

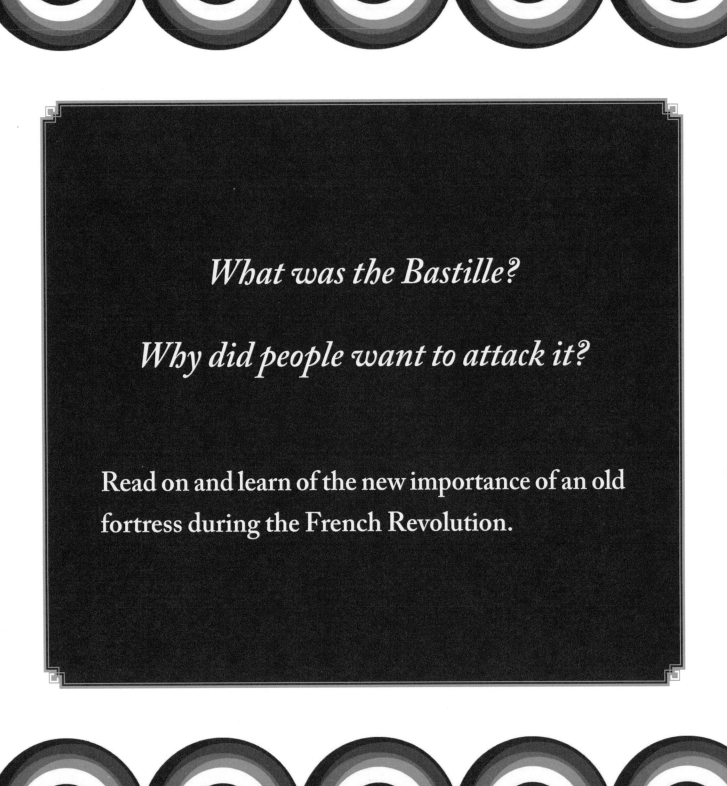

What was the Bastille?

Why did people want to attack it?

Read on and learn of the new importance of an old
fortress during the French Revolution.

THE EVE OF REVOLUTION

In 1789 in France, there was widespread unhappiness. Drought and bad planning had led to several years of poor harvests, and even basic food like bread was very expensive.

Bastille, 1789

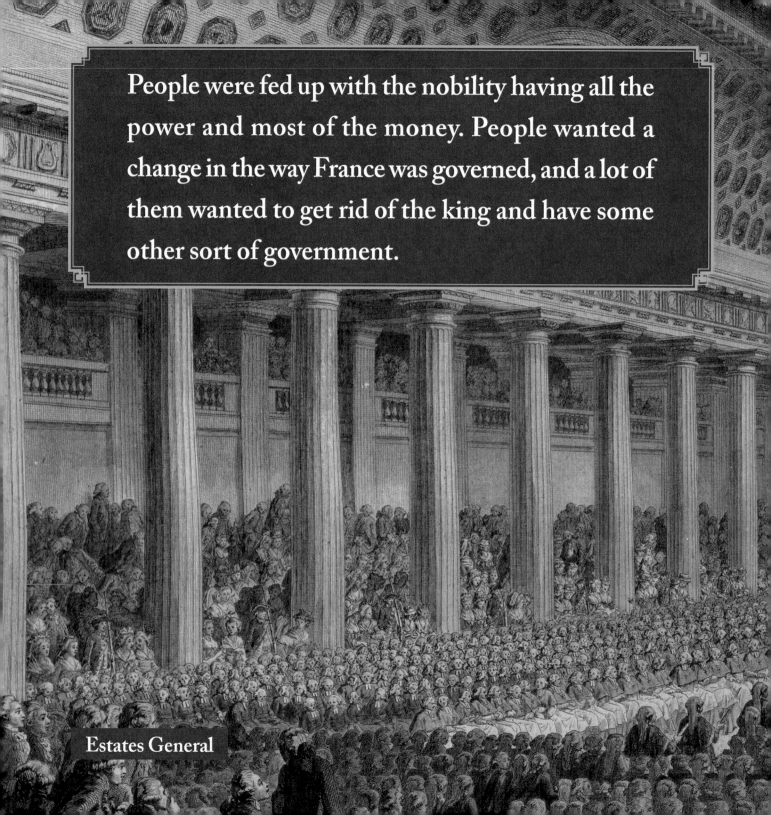

People were fed up with the nobility having all the power and most of the money. People wanted a change in the way France was governed, and a lot of them wanted to get rid of the king and have some other sort of government.

Estates General

King Louis XVI convened the Estates-General to approve new taxes, but the body declared itself the National Assembly and started to write a new constitution for France. Louis went along with some efforts of the National Assembly, but made some other moves, like dismissing a popular minister, that made people more angry. Riots started in Paris and other centers, with people making equal demands for bread and for human rights.

National Assembly

Palace of Versailles

The king was at his palace at Versailles, about 12 miles outside Paris, and the National Assembly was working there. But the center of the popular uprising was in the capital, Paris. Leaders of the movement to change the government in France stirred the crowds up to violent acts. They looked for opportunities for action that would catch people's attention, and they began to focus on the Bastille.

WHAT WAS THE BASTILLE?

The Bastille was a fortification (a "bastide") first built in 1370 as part of the defences of Paris against attacks from outside the city, mainly by the English during the Thirty Years' War.

Bastille

Bastille Courtyard

It was expanded many times until it was a fortress that could defend aganst attacks from any direction. It was over one hundred feet high, and had a moat around it that was 80 feet wide to make it harder for people to reach the walls or the gates. You could see the top of the Bastille from almost anywhere in Paris.

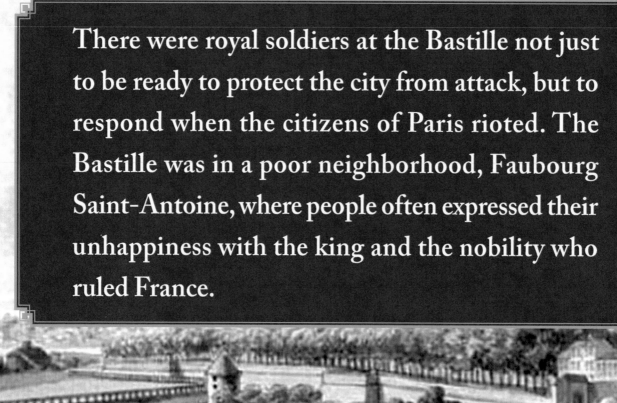

There were royal soldiers at the Bastille not just to be ready to protect the city from attack, but to respond when the citizens of Paris rioted. The Bastille was in a poor neighborhood, Faubourg Saint-Antoine, where people often expressed their unhappiness with the king and the nobility who ruled France.

Bastille

Bastille

A FORTRESS-PRISON

In the late 1400s part of the Bastille started to be used as a prison, mainly for political enemies, spies, and members of the nobility who had committed fraud or other money-related crimes. Most of the people held there were arrested by direct order of the king, and were prisoners without ever having a trial or even going before a judge.

By the 1700s there were rarely more than thirty prisoners in the Bastille, and many were far from ordinary prisoners. The philosopher Voltaire spent time in the Bastille—twice! Others held there were political activists, journalists who wrote article critical of the nobility, people who criticized the Roman Catholic Church, and those the king was angry with, like General Charles Dumouriez. One economist said that spending six months in the Bastille for writing about the nobility helped to make his fortune: sales of his books increased greatly, and his name became widely known so that he had work waiting for him when he was released.

Voltaire

King Louis XVI

LETTRES DE CACHET

The kings of France had the power to jail people just by writing a "lettre de cachet". People became outraged that one man should have such power, and the Bastille, where such prisoners were often held, became a symbol of all that was wrong with the power of kings. King Louis XVI made things worse in 1787 when he used lettres de cachet to imprison two leaders of the Paris government and a general, the Duke of Orleans. There were huge demonstrations against these "acts of a tyrant".

TROUBLED TIMES

In 1789, the Estates General, the body the king had called together to approve new taxes, turned into an independent body, the National Assembly.

Estates General

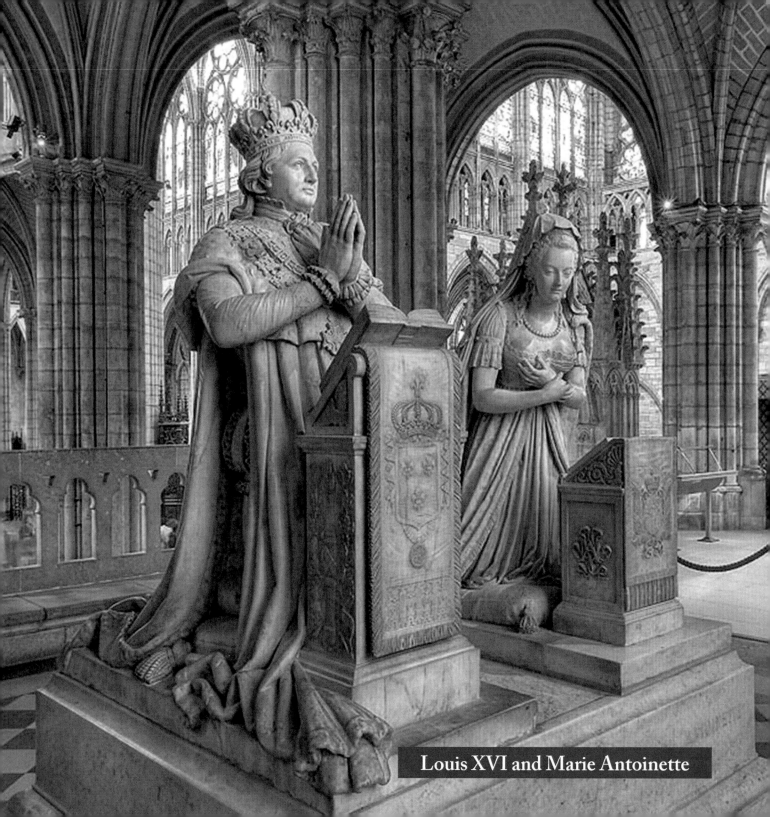

Louis XVI and Marie Antoinette

Some in this body wanted to change the government of France to be like that of England, where there was a strong parliament and a king with limited powers. Others in the assembly wanted more radical change, including the end of the monarchy.

Bad harvests and bad government decisions had caused the price of bread to rise steeply, and working class families were spending most of their income just on the most basic food. This added to the outrage against the small group of nobility and rich landowners who had most of the money and power in France.

Then Louis XVI made two moves that made things worse. He assembled royal troops in several areas around Paris, and near Versailles, where he lived and where the National Assembly was meeting. He also dismissed his finance minister, who was popular, and replaced him with a very conservative man who was opposed to any change. People started to attend demonstrations, that sometimes turned into riots. They were afraid the king was going to try to use the army to gain back power he had lost to the National Assembly.

JULY 12

On July 12, a huge crowd gathered to demand the return of the finance minister. A royal cavalry regiment attacked the crowd, forcing it to scatter for a while, but it reformed.

Storming of the Bastille

The French Guard, the garrison of Paris, was ordered to force the crowd to disperse, but the soldiers refused to open fire. Many of the Guard actually went to join the protest, taking their weapons with them!

Groups attacked and burned 40 customs houses, where taxes were collected, and forced officials to flee the city. Other groups tried to gather any weapons they could find, expecting the king's troops to attack.

Le Marquis de Launay

JULY 13

The normal garrison of the Bastille in peacetime was only about 80 soldiers. Its governor, de Launay, had requested additional troops earlier in July, but there were fewer than 200 troops in the fortress. Its main strength was its massive walls.

On July 13, crowds, many with muskets and other weapons looted from small armories around the city, gathered near the Bastille, which had closed its gates and raised its drawbridges. People started shooting at the soldiers on the walls. The soldiers started firing back.

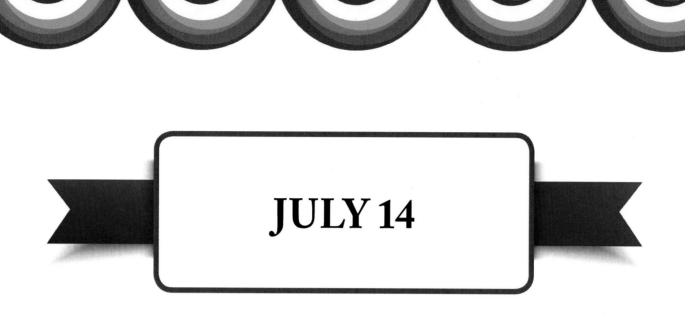

JULY 14

The next day, an even larger crowd gathered, with many more muskets. They demanded that de Launay surrender the Bastille to them, and he refused.

Some revolutionaries managed to get over the outer wall of the Bastille and lower one of the drawbridges. More than three hundreds revolutionaries got into the main area of the Bastille. The commandant, de Launay, ordered his troops to fire as the mob tried to lower the second drawbridge. More than a hundred people died.

Fighting continued and the mob set fires where they could. Around 3 pm, soldiers who had deserted from the army and joined the revolutionary mob arrived. They were hidden by the smoke, and were able to drag five small cannon into place and aim them at the Bastille before the defenders knew what was going on.

When de Launay learned of this development, he decided the fight could not be won and surrendered the Bastille. The mob seized weapons and gunpowder from the Bastille, freed the prisoners (there were only seven!), and took de Launay and his men to the Hotel de Ville, the headquarters of the Paris government to be put on trial

Hotel de Ville

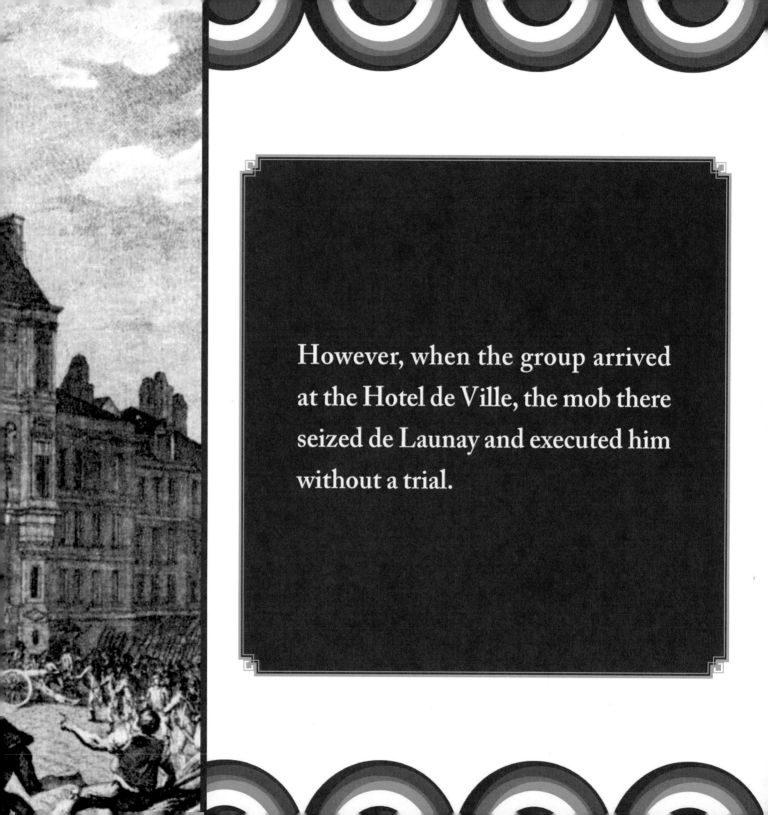

However, when the group arrived at the Hotel de Ville, the mob there seized de Launay and executed him without a trial.

WHAT HAPPENED NEXT

The new revolutionary government of France ordered that the Bastille be torn down. By February, 1790, its walls were completely gone.

The capture of the Bastille gave momentum to the young French Revolution. Revolutionaries took control of Paris, much of the countryside, the government and, eventually the royal family.

In itself, the Bastille was not an important strong point if the king were going to have a war with the revolutionaries. But as a symbol, it was very important. It was a sign that the power of the old order—the king and his family, the nobility, the rich landowners, and the the senior members of the Roman Catholic Church in France—was coming to an end. The fact that not even the army would stand in support of the king showed that Louis XVI, and through him the whole system of government by kings, had lost the confidence of France.

Bastille Day

Even today July 14, Bastille Day, is a major French national holiday.

THE AMAZING FRENCH REVOLUTION

The French Revolution began in 1789 and continued until 1798. Do you know the men and women on both sides of the struggle, and what they did? To learn more, read Baby Professor books like The French Revolution: People Power in Action, Moms Needed Bread!, The Marquis de Lafayette: The Hero of Two Worlds, Marie Antoinette and her Lavish Parties, and They Got Involved: Famous People during the French Revolution.

A cart laden with casualties during the French Revolution